MAHATMA JYOTIRAO PHULE: REFORMER OF INDIAN EDUCATION

Dr. Ismail Thamarasseri, *Assistant Professor, School of Pedagogical Sciences, Mahatma Gandhi University, Kottayam, Kerala, India, PIN: 686560, E-mail: ismailktkl@gmail.com*

Dr. Gawher Ahmad Bhat, *Assistant Professor (Teacher Education), School of Education, Central University of Kashmir, Ganderbal, PIN: 191201, J&K, India*

Imtiyaz Ahmad Hajam, *Former M.Ed. Student, School of Education, Central University of Kashmir, Ganderbal, PIN: 191201, J&K, India*

ABSTRACT

Mahatma Jyotiraio Phule (1827-1890) was among one of the modern educational philosophers of Maharashtra who played an eminent role in the development of education in Maharashtra, especially for the education of backward classes and women in late nineteenth century. His studies explore the Brahminical supremacy and hegemonies in the social setup of Indian society in general and Maharastrian society in particular. This book is an attempt to highlight the crucial role played by Mahatma Jyotiraio Phule in the field of education and welfare of backward classes.

Key words: Education, Maharastra, Mahatma Jyotirao Govind Rao Phule, India

Introduction

Mahatma Jyotirao Govind Rao Phule was born in satara district of Maharashtra on 11th April 1827. He was from a family, that belonged to the agricultural caste, traditionally occupied as gardeners and considered to be one of the Shudras varna in the ritual ranking system of Hinduism. His original surname was Gorhay and he belonged to Mali caste. His grandfather Shetiba Gorhay was engaged in selling flowers, garlands and flower decorations at religious and family functions at Pune. As Jyotirao's two uncles were served as florists under Peshwas, their family become popular as 'Phule', the flower man. Jyotirao's father Govindrao was also engaged in family business and his mother Chimnabai died when he was only nine months old and he had one elder brother.

His Education

During his time higher education was not accessible to lower castes, he was himself belonging to a lower caste (Mali), the Mali caste was not participating in education and only attending primary schooling to learn the basics of reading, writing and basic arithmetic was popular. After his basic schooling, he joined his family work and started working in farms and shop. After the influence of Christian Missionary, his father allowed Jyotirao to attend local Scottish Mission's High School run by Murray Mitchell. Jyotirao completed his English schooling in 1847. At the age of 13, he was married to Savitribai as chosen by his father. The year 1848, was a turning point of his life, when he attended the wedding of a Brahmin friend, he was rebuked and insulted by his friend's parents, as Jyotirao belonged to lower caste. As per customs during those days, lower castes were not actively allowed to participate in Brahmin's marriages and other social functions. After this incident, he realized the injustice faced by caste system to the different lower castes and took an oath to organize the lower classes through spread of education and awakening and also to create a new social order. He inspired the Shudras and Ati-Shudras to fight united against caste dogmas and social oppression. His attack on Brahmin domination, social evils, orthodoxy, ignorance, illiteracy and all the oppressive features of the Varna-based Hinduism had made him a historic figure. Jyotirao read the book 'Rights of Man' written by Thomas Paine which influence him very much and developed a keen sense of social justice. Phule had read biographies of George Washington and Chhatrapti Shivaji. They were source of inspiration for him. He realized that "lower castes" and women were at a disadvantage in Indian society, and also that education of these sections was vital to their emancipation. Phule was influenced by the books and based on his observation in society, in place of exploitative Indian social order, he wanted to establish a society founded on principles of Individual liberty and equality and in place of Hinduism he would have like to put universal religion.

His priority was education of women and lower castes. Hence at home he began educating his wife Savitribai and opened a girls' school in August 1848. The orthodox opponents of Jyotirao Phule were furious and they started a vicious campaign against him. He refused to be unnerved by their malicious propaganda. As no teacher dared to work in a school in which untouchables were admitted as students. Phule asked his wife to teach the girls in his school. Stones and brickbats were thrown at her when she was on her way to school. The reactionaries threatened Jyotirao's father with dire consequences if he did not dissociate from his son's activities. Yielding to the pressure, Jyotirao's father asked his son and daughter-in-law to leave his house as both of them refused to give up their noble endeavour.

Jyotirao's father, Govind Rao Phule, being a man of tradition, was deeply troubled by his son's actions. However, Govind Rao friends of the same caste convinced him that Jyotirao was right in taking action against age-old Hindu religious beliefs. Jyotirao argued with his father but to no avail. Govindrao in a fit of anger told his son to go his own way and ordered Jyotirao and his wife to leave his house. Jyotirao's wife, Savitribai, stood by her husband in this period of trial. Thus, Jyotirao and his wife moved out. Meanwhile the school closed down temporarily due to lack of sufficient funds. When the finances improved somewhat, Jytorao reopened the school in the space donated by his friend. Mahatma Jyotirao Phule continued with his mission. On the 3rd July, 1851, he founded a girls' school in which eight girls were admitted on the first day. Dadoba Pandurang Tarkhadkar was the supervisor of the local government schools. On 16 October 1851, he inspected the first school set up by Jytorao in Budhwar Peth. He remarked that it went to the credit of those who ran the school which had made such remarkable progress in short span of time. Meanwhile, Jyotirao set up a library for his students, since he felt that a library is an important means of imparting education. The number of students in Jyotirao's school grew ten times more than that in government schools. This amazing transformation was due to the excellent conditions present and the conducive atmosphere for teaching. On 16 November 1852 the government called a meeting of local leaders in Vishram Wada to felicitate Jyotirao. On behalf of the government, Jyotirao was honoured with a shawl - an honour hitherto conferred only on Brahmins. Steadily the number of students increased. Savitribai taught in this school also and had to suffer a lot because of the hostility of the orthodox people. Jyotirao opened two more schools for girls during 1851-52. Although, he was hard put to it to make both ends meet, he did not neglect the schoolwork. His wife faithfully supported him. In 1855, Jyotirao Phule brought to light the beliefs and rituals practiced in the name of God. Some educated Hindus too were fighting against superstitions in order to bring about new thinking. It was being realized that Jyotirao Phule actions and teachings not only challenged the superiority of the Brahmins but struck at the very root of Hindu religion. Some fanatics, disturbed at this, sent some assassins to get rid of Jyotirao Phule. But when the assassins set feet in Jyotirao Phule house, they entered into a dialogue with him. Jyotirao Phule asked them. "Why have you come to kill me? What wrong have I done to you?" The assassins replied. "We are going to be paid a thousand rupees each for the job". Jyotirao replied, "Alright, then here is my neck. I know it is your poverty which in making you do this." Jyotirao Phule magnanimity impressed the assassins.

Jyotirao opted for government service, he would have prospered but he chose public service as he considered it his moral duty towards society. He engaged in private business to support his family. When the government drew up a plan for the construction of the Khadakvasala dam, Jyotirao along with his friend Sakharam Paranjape, acquired the contract for the supply of stone. In this line of business, Jyotirao came into contact with workers and government officials, especially engineers. Concerned about the welfare of the workers, Jyotirao fought for their rights. He impressed upon them the value of education for their children. He became a staunch critic of corrupt practices in such business enterprises.

Jyotirao's chief aim was to strike at the social structure. Towards this end he was determined to remove ignorance, illiteracy, prejudices and caste-based beliefs among the lower castes and free them from the mental slavery resulting from centuries of Brahmin dominance. In 1872 he wrote the book, Gulamgiri (Slavery). He remarked in his book that "The Shudras are the life of this nation. In times of economic and political crises the government should rely on them rather than on the Brahmins. If care is taken to ensure that the Shudras are kept happy and contented, the government will have no cause for doubting their loyalty". Hence, he fought for the rights of Shudras in society against Brahmin created rituals and practices.

He has said that he is doing a fair amount of contributions for the access to the education, but it seems the Government is ignorant of the condition of Shudras and Ati-Shudras. Phule represents his critical views on the educational policy of Government. Throughout the pages of his document, he emphasizes that how the benefits of education are being enjoyed by only the people belonging to upper castes. The British Indian Government was the hope for the lower caste people as it was the only political force that could fight against the Brahmanism. Education was entirely dominated by Brahmins. In his ideas on the education, Phule had also stressed the English education for lower castes.

In this way, he is mainly exposing how the dominance of upper castes operates in the tract of education. He proposes the plan for the amendment in the education system. In his proposal, he puts forward also the idea of scholarships which will be helpful for the masses to acquire the education. Without scholarships, the lower classes will further be excluded again due to their poverty. He also asks for the increase in the number of schools, for remodelling the teachers and the method of teaching in the schools. The lower-class people feel alienated in the school because of the Brahmin teachers. In other words, Phule mainly recommended conceptualizing the system of education, so it may be fruitful to all the groups of people in society, not just to Brahmins. In the vision of Phule, the education was not only for the lower castes but also for the women. In fact, he educated his own wife, Savtribai Phule. Savtribai was the main leader of women's education as she was the first woman teacher who founded "the first school" for females. Both Jyotirao Phule and Savtribai Phule are considered as the pioneers of women's education organizations. They both worked together to liberate women from patriarchy and untouchability. They opened several girl schools.

Marriage system in society was based on age old orthodox traditions. Widow Remarriage was banned and child marriage was very common among Brahmins and other upper castes in the Hindu society. Many widows were young and not all of them could live in a manner in which the orthodox people expected them to live. Some of the delinquent widows resorted to abortion or left their illegitimate children to their fate by leaving them on the streets. Out of pity for the orphans, Jyotirao Phule established an orphanage, possibly the first such institution founded by an Indian, Jyotirao gave protection to pregnant widows and assured them that the orphanage would take care of their children. It was in this orphanage run by Jyotirao that a Brahmin widow gave birth to a boy in 1873 and Phule adopted him as his son and he was named as Yeshwant Phule.

Jyotirao had set a personal example of his belief in the eradication of untouchability. Paying no heed to the orthodox dictates of Hindu society, Jyotirao threw open the water tank near his house to untouchables, for whom the municipality had not made any arrangements for providing water. During summer, they had to walk long distances to fetch water. Jyotirao's caste fellows threatened to ostracize him.

Foundation of Satya Shodhak Samaj

Mahatma Jyotirao Phule founded the Satya Shodhak Samaj (Society of the Seekers of Truth) in 1873, for the uplift of lower castes and to prevent their exploitation by Brahmins and the upper castes. Membership of the Samaj was open to all castes. Brahmins, Mahars, Mangs and others were members of the Samaj. Wherever branches of the Samaj were opened, meetings were held every week. Rationality and the equality were the principles on which he based the Satya Shodhak Samaj. The former principle was used to overthrow tradition and deny the supremacy of the scriptures. The principle of equality was used to attack the caste system. The Satya Shodhak Samaj worked to undermine the cultural and religious sanction for priest hood by conducting rituals and ceremonies without Brahmins. In its attack on the caste system it drew from both Western rationalism as well as indigenous sources of social revolt like the Bhakti. What distinguished the Satya Shodhak Samaj was its non-elitist mass nature. In propagating its ideology, it made wide use of the vernacular. The backbone it is came from the Maratha peasantry (Maratha Kunbis, Malis, Kolis etc.). It also gained some support from untouchables. The "commercial bourgeoisie" comprising of tradesmen, contractors etc. were another source of support.

The activities of the Satya Shodhak Samaj got a fillip when the Shahu Maharaja of Kolhapur extended his support to it. The Maharaja had realized that political power was also necessary for advancement of the backward classes. To this end he encouraged the education of the lower castes and introduced reservation for them in his administration. Following Mahatma Phule he aided in replacing religious ceremonies which previously were the prerogative of

Brahmins by those performed by the lower castes themselves. Brahmins who were the main losers in the new dispensation were the most vocal in condemning the Kolhapur experiment. In 1876, there were 316 members of the Satya Shodhak Samaj. Jyotirao refused to regard the Vedas as sacrosanct. He opposed idolatry and denounced the *Chaturvarna* system. In 1876, Jyotirao was nominated as a member of the Poona Municipality. He tried to help the people in the famine-stricken areas of Maharashtra when a severe famine in 1877 forced people in rural areas to leave their villages.

In 1882, Phule wrote a long statement to the Hunter Commission on Education in India. In this political piece of writing, Phule appeals the Government to reform the system of education because the educational policy is not reaching to the masses (to the lower castes). He endorsed the idea that education should be made available to the masses. Phule also focuses on the idea of primary education which, he thinks, should be made compulsory till the age of twelve.

After founding the Satya Shodhak Samaj, Jyotirao set out to put into practice the aims and goals of the Samaj. He invited applications for scholarships which he awarded to ten students; this was much acclaimed. The Samaj performed several marriages without availing the services of Brahmins. The bride and the groom were made to pledge loyalty to each other and the marriage party then blessed the couple. As can be imagined, a wedding without a Brahmin priest was at the time an-unheard-of event.

In 1875, farmers from Ahmedabad, Pune, Satara, and Sholapur rose in revolt against the money-lenders who had been defrauding the poor by making them sign bonds worth more than the loan advanced. The government appointed a committee to investigate into the matter. On the committee's recommendation, the government passed the Deccan Agricultural Relief Act, with a view to improve relations between the money-lenders and the farmers. There were provisions to ensure that the bonds were bonafide and the rights of the farmers were protected. Jyotirao's weekly, *Deenbandhu* supported these regulations. Towards, the end of 1879, Jyotirao began to press the government, through the *Deenbandhu*, for introducing compulsory primary education. He persisted with his demand, but did not receive any response from the government. Jyotirao was deeply concerned at the workers' problems. His associate, Narayanrao, wrote on workers' problems in the *Deenbandhu* realizing peasants' problems, he wrote 'Shetakaryacha Aasud' book in 1883. It revealed that, man's primary needs are directed at the production of food and clothing. Hence, it is important for the farmer community to be healthy and strong. Modern society has been built on the industrial revolution but it still requires the support to its foundation from the farmer community. At present there are three kinds of farmers - the Surdra, farmers or Kunbis, the Malis and the Dhangars. Those who originally made a living from farming alone were the Kulwadis or the Kunbis, those who cultivated gardens apart from their farms, were the Malis, those who did both and raised sheep and goats in addition were the Dhangars. Jyotirao's good work in the Pune municipality continued unabated. In June 1890, Hari Raoji Chiplunkar put forth the resolution that the election of the acting committee of the municipality should be held by a vote from all members, before the commencement of every working year. Jyotirao supported this resolution. Conscious of the welfare of the public he believed that the resolution would prevent power from being concentrated in the hands of anyone group. He displayed exemplary courage in his conviction when the municipality voted for approval of the expenses to be borne by it during Viceroy Lord Lytton's impending visit to Pune. Jyotirao Phule wrote thirty-three articles in the Sarvajanik Satyadharma, which define the rules for the creation of a world-family based on basic human rights as well as the social and intellectual attitudes essential for it. The gist of these articles, in more or less Phule's words, is as follows:

- All men and women should live together unite on this earth as one family, with honesty and without discrimination, no matter to which village, province, country, continent or religious beliefs they adhere to.
- The Creator created man to be independent and capable of enjoying equal rights as others.

- The Creator has given freedom to all men and women to express themselves freely, but without causing harm on account of their thoughts or views. This is known as true (righteous) conduct.
- Conduct which will please the Creator is public truth (virtue). The honest behaviour of any human being towards his fellow human beings may be termed as morality.
- Charity: Only if they receive charity will the Creator be truly happy.

It is quite clear that these are the thoughts of one who believed in a democratic society.

- Jyotirao borrowed the concept of the Kingdom of God on earth from Christianity, although he introduced the new concept of human values. He was not a nationalist. In his opinion, the term 'nation' was to be interpreted as 'the community of a region, based on freedom and equality'. He says time and again that groups of communities bound by the Caste or religion does not constitute a nation. A religious community should always remain a constituent of the world community. Religious institutions have led to separatism. He warns repeatedly against blind beliefs in religion.
- 'Nirmik', meaning God, is the new term Jyotirao has used for the Creator of the universe. He believed that terms hitherto coined for God, had grown out of practices and observances, of prayer or worship, which only created social rift amongst human beings.

Hence, he avoided terms such as Ishwar, Allah, Brahma, etc, according to him, service to mankind or defending human equality and freedom was in essence the true worship of God.

Works of Mahatma JyotiraoPhule:

Apart from educational, welfare activities, eradication of untouchability and emphasizing human rights of all classes of people, Mahatma Phule has written few of the notable works by expressing his ideas. They are as under:

- **Trutiya Ratna (1855):** This drama is considered as the first modern, social and independent play in Marathi, 'knowledge' is considered as the third jewel in Indian tradition. In this sense, the title is appropriate. This drama depicts how 'Bhats' (Brahmins) exploit ignorant Shudras. On the other hand, this drama deposits a Christian preacher shows the exploited Shudras, the way of truth. This drama effectively depicts the importance of education by illustrating how the masses are cheated because of their ignorance.
- **Brahmnanche Kasab (1869):** The exploitation of ignorant and poor Shurdas by 'Bhats' (Brahmins) has been presented in poetic form.
- **Gulamgiri (1873):** Mythical stories have been critically analysed. The fight between Aryas and the original 'Kshetrapatis' has been effectively described. For the first time, it has been presented that; "Indian history is the history of the fight between Brahmins and Non-Brahmins".
- **Shekaryach Aasud (1883):** Jyotirao had studied the poor condition of the Shudras and Ati-Shudras from several indigenous and foreign books. He has presented all those ideas together in this book.
- **Satsaar:** Jyotirao had published 'Satsaar' (journal) in two parts, and the following subjects have been presented; Brahma Samaj; Prarthana Samaj; Social Status of infants born of persons from different castes; Ideology of the Aryabhattas; in the second part, Jyotirao has severally condemned the people who used to criticize the women for adopting the new ways.
- **Ishara:** Jyotirao has specified that the caste imbalance is the obstacle in the development of the nation. Jyotirao warned that, false opinions can misguide the common people ultimately this would harm the Nation. Jyotirao has indicated

that, the statement, "the condition of the farmers is better is false".

- **Sarvajanik Satyadharma (1891):** This is the last book by Jyotirao. It was published posthumously in the year 1891. Jyotirao completed the writing of this book with his left hand, as his right hand was paralyzed. Apart from his notable works, he has also submitted many of the requisitions and reports to the Government even which are available now. Throughout his life, Jyotirao Phule fought for the emancipation of the downtrodden people and the struggle, which he launched at a young age ended only when he died on 28th November, 1890. After Jyotirao's death in 1890, there was a period of lull, when the flame lit by Jyotirao waned. The Satya Shodhak Samaj movement was totally a social movement and nothing to do with the politics, but the members of Satya Shodhak Samaj dissolved Satya Shodhak Samaj and merged it with Congress party in 1930.

Later in the twentieth century, Phule came to be acknowledged as the "Guru" of Dr. Ambedkar. The November of 1890 marked the Phule's death and Dr. Ambedkar's birth was marked with April 1891. Dr. B. R. Ambedkar is a brilliant figure from our Indian history. Dr. Babasaheb Ambedkar achieved the highest education, becoming well-versed in all the subjects.

When the biographical sketch of Mahatma Phule is analyzed, it is found that, his life was noble as he faced many of the difficulties in the protection and assurance of human rights of backward classes, Shudras, Ati-Shudras and women. Due to his aim, he lost support of many of his well-wishers especially, his own father and many of the friends. Still, Mahatma Phule dedicated his life towards the empowerment and development of these downtrodden classes. Education is major solution as stated by Phule to solve the problems of these classes. Realizing this truth, he encouraged education of the masses.

Social Contributions of Mahatma Phule

Jyotirao Phule (1827-1890) initiated social change in nineteenth century India especially in Maharashtra through his philosophy. The nineteenth century was an era of social criticism and transformation that focused on nationalism, caste and gender. All major questions taken up by the reformers were connected with women's issues such as female infanticide, child marriage, ban on women's education, Sati, tonsuring of widows, ban on widow remarriage etc. At the same time, reformers concentrated more on reforming the social institutions of family and marriage with special emphasis on the status and rights of women. Jyotirao took up the issue of gender and caste. He revolted against the unjust caste-system under which millions of people had suffered for centuries. His revolt against the caste system integrated social and religious reform with equality. He emerged as the unchanged leader of the depressed classes in Maharashtra and was recognized as a leader of downtrodden class in all over India. He was influenced by American thinker Thomas Paine's ideas of *Rights of Man*.

Jyotirao Phule (1827-1890) one of the *"Mahatmas'* (Great Soul) of India, occupies a unique position among social reformers of Maharashtra in the nineteenth century India. He was first teacher of oppressed, critic of orthodoxy in the social system after Buddha and a revolutionary. The task of bringing concerning socio-religious reform in nineteenth century was not so simple. Social reformers had made tremendous effort for social and religious change in Indian society during this period. Phule played a remarkable role in this area. In order to remedy the problems of gender and caste oppression, he contributed with a constructive suggestion. This was by way of a new image of religion which was known as universal religion. He started reflecting critically about the ground realities of the huge majority of rural masses. He read broadly on American Democracy, the French revolution and was stuck by the logical way of thinking in Thomas Paine's "Rights of Man". Influenced by Thomas Paine's book on "Rights of Man",

(1791), Phule developed a keen sense of social justice, becoming passionately critical of handicap caste system.

Women Emancipation and Empowerment

Jyotirao Phule had done a remarkable work for the emancipation of women. He raised the problem of women's oppression and his thoughts on resolving women's oppression through their own efforts and autonomy makes him join the company of other nineteenth century Western Philosophers and male feminists like J.S. Mill and F. Engels. Mahatma Phule was a symbol of the revolution of social equality which was born of the impact of Western education and the great idea of equality brought by it to India. Equality as a force began to make for social, economic and national change all over India. In India the threads of religion were lock stitched into the social and economic privileges of the few. That socio-religious system called the caste system bred inequality.

Jyotirao Phule started women education from the education of his wife and trained her for the school. Mahatma Jyotirao Phule and Savitribai, were remarkable personalities, especially for their times. Savitribai was the first women teacher in India. Jyotirao Phule started the first school for girls at Pune, in the year 1848. He advocated education for female students from the downtrodden (Shudras/ AtiShudras) communities and adults. He established institutes like the 'Pune Female Native Schools' and the 'Society for Promoting Education for Mahar, Mangs'. More important, he engaged in his education at home too. Jyotirao prepared his wife, Savitribai, to teach in the girls' school, with a view to educating the women first, in order to bring in the value of equality at home. Savitribai had to face bitter opposition from the orthodox society of the time for teaching girls and people from the under privileged groups in the school. Despite this bitter opposition, Jyotirao and Savitribai continued their work with sincerity. Women empowerment is an essential concept these days as Y.V. Satyanarayana rightly said, "The dominance of men over women is an age-old practice, but after the advent of democracy and democratic institution, almost every nation recognized the freedom, equality, and human rights of women. Now, women are entitled to live with self-respect and dignity by exercising various rights to women in the past and its ongoing effects in the present should be properly addressed by way of empowering women in all spheres of social life".

They focused on providing education to both girls and boys that was to be vocational and trade-oriented in nature, to make their students self-reliant and capable of independent thought. In the 1852 report, they expressed the following opinion. An industrial department should be attached to the schools where children could learn useful trades and crafts and be able, after leaving school, to manage their lives comfortably and independently. Mahatma Jyotirao Phule's bold efforts to educate women, Shudras and the untouchables had deep effect on the values, beliefs and ideologies. His efforts unleashed the forces of awakening among the common masses. Education made women more knowledgeable. They became conscious of what is right and wrong in the light of science. Women began to question the age-old customs which degraded them.

Phule knew that besides illiteracy, there were many social evils in the society, which have crippled the whole social order. It was all due to ignorance, superstitions and traditional prejudicial thinking. In those days' widow's problem was there in the society. It was a great curse in the Hindu social system. Due to early child marriage and many other social reasons those unfortunate women who lived as widows were not allowed to remarry. The dominating upper castes and the ruling chiefs even encouraged Sati tradition, against which foremost social reformer Raja Ram Mohan Roy raised his voice.

As practical reformer, Phule virtually destroyed all religious dogmas that were against reason and opened the door to reforms. His aim was to reconstruct society on the basis of equality, liberty and reason. Although the problem of remarriage of widows was confined to Brahmins and some other high caste Hindus, Phule was moved by the miserable condition of the widows, and often by their immoral behaviour. Sometimes they were involved in child murder. A man of flaming indignation against injustice, Jyotirao actively supported the movement for widow remarriage. He wanted to liberate the woman from her age-old shackles.

Emancipation and Welfare of Backward Classes

The history of nineteenth century is the story of the impetus for social reform in which the introduction and spread of modern education was an important element. Schools which taught English language were opened not so much to educate the masses but to groom Indian people to run the British government. Christian missionaries opened a Marathi school in Pune for the public. During this transitional phase, even though education was open to masses, the common people were not aware of its importance. Jyotirao had worked for the masses and made them aware of education as a vehicle for social change. 19th Century was a period of social problems like *Varna* system, mythology, caste-system, ignorance about human rights etc. In oppressed castes great-grandparents and grand-parents did their community work which involved hard-menial labour. Social mobility was not permissible for them. They were not even aware of their rights; illiteracy was very high in the society. Jyotirao shows the light of hope, to free from these problems of society. He revolted against the unjust caste-system and upheld the cause of education of women and lower castes. He started primary education and higher education and fought for their rights. Thus, he ushered in primary education as a tool in perceiving the work of the oppressed castes as dignified labour that was exploited by society. In 20th Century people belongs to oppressed castes their parents had opportunity to get undergraduate education which they could also impart to their children. This was a period when oppressed castes struggled to enter institutions and make their presence visible in the context of nation-building. It was also a period when they had an understanding of their rights and responsibilities.

In the late 20th century and the beginning of 21st Century oppressed castes to an extent have entered into institutions of higher learning and have started producing knowledge that questions inequality and reconstructs identity from the theoretical point of view. They are ready to face the challenges of their time. We can see the growth of education from 19th to 21st century India. 19th century the focus on primary to higher education, then in 20th century system focused on Under-graduate level education, and now in 21st century high level research on social sciences is available for the generation. The present position is better because of education which has given them self-respect, made them aware of their rights, organizations to voice their feelings.

During those days the Shudras and the untouchables were dehumanized a lot not only in Maharashtra but whole of India. Phule's social and political ideology was totally revolutionary suggesting deep involvement with social transformation. People belonging to lower classes whether touchable or untouchable Shudras, they were all treated like slaves and serfs. Though the renaissance had begun, but the Shudras were hated and discouraged to participate in the social life of the country. Virtually they had no right to education. No social status. They were not allowed to use public places, visit temples take water from public wells and tanks. He revolted against the unjust caste-system under which millions of people had suffered for centuries. The Dalit at that time did not have any political, social, educational and economic rights. He condemned dual morality of the Brahman system. He said equal opportunity should get to all people. He said by birth all are free and equal. All human beings have natural rights. He was a militant advocate of human rights to the downtrodden. A pioneer of anti-caste movement, he was no doubt, the leading social reformer who founded and started non-Brahmin movement which reawakened the Mangs, Mahars, Chambhars, Kumbhar, Kolis, Koshtis, Kunbis, Malis, Ramoshis etc., the dehumanized castes of 19th century Maharashtra, through Satya Shodhak Samaj founded in 1873. For long the Hindu scriptures and the Manusmriti prevented the Shudras and the Ati-Shudras the tight of education and a just place in the Hindu social order.

Phule said that the main aim of Satya Shodhak Samaj was to save die lower classes from the clutches of the hydo-critical Brahmins and their totally false and opportunistic so-called scriptures, by fighting untouchability and caste system which had weakened and enslaved India. His Satya Shodhak Samaj discarded the religious services of the priestly class. He advised his people to start priest less marriages and even in other religious ceremonies priests should not be invited. In the rural areas the Shudras and Ati-Shudras, artisans and peasants were exploited and suppressed by both Bhatji (priest) and Shetji (money lender or trader). Phule in his writings and speeches exposed the fraudulent practices of these classes. Jyotirao Phule protested against man-made inequality which was rooted in Hindu caste-system and Varna-Vyavastha. He struggled fearlessly to implement the reforms in the Hindu society. He tried to remove inferiority complex from the minds of the people. He made Shudras aware. He advised them to take education and acquire power; they are not slave but human beings.

As T.L. Joshi said, "Jyotirao Phule was one of the first persons to rebel against the traditional social system in India. From where did he find the inspiration for this revolt considering that the prevailing social laws had taken a firm hold on the Indian mind for thousands of years? The answer is that Jyotirao was a Satyashodhak - a seeker of truth - the moral truth of human life. The manifestation of that perennial truth was his belief in man's freedom in the universe, as upheld by modern western civilisation". He stressed upon education because illiteracy was the root cause of the degradation of lower castes, as stated previously. "Mahatma Jyotirao Phule stressed on universalization of education i.e. education for all irrespective of caste, colour, creed, sex and poverty. Mahatma Jyotirao Phule had done a lot in his life to reform society, to fight for establishing equality in society.

Educational Philosophy of Jyotira Phule

The history of nineteenth century is the story of the impetus for social reform in which the introduction and spread of modern education was an important element. Phule believed in overthrowing the social system in which man has been deliberately made dependent on others, illiterate, ignorant and poor, with a view to exploiting him. To him blind faith eradication formed part of a broad socio-economic transformation. This was his strategy for ending exploitation of human beings. Mere advice, education and alternative ways of living are not enough, unless the economic framework of exploitation comes to an end. Shudras became conscious of their caste identity and started claiming equality with higher castes in all areas of life. In short, Mahatma Jyotiba Phule liberated women and Shudras from the control of religious vested interests and laid the foundation for a Backward Class Movement in India". Jyotirao Phule established two schools in 1851 for girls. A third school was started by him in 1852. These were the first girl schools started by Indians in Pune, where the *Presbyterian Mission* had already founded such schools several years ago. In March 1852, Phule founded the *Poona Low Caste School*. On the eve of the public examination, a correspondent of *The Poona Observer and Deccan Weekly Reporter* in its issue of March 19, 1853, stated that the origin and progress of the school was owing to the individual labour of Phule who taught the students of the first class in this school while the other three lower classes were taught by different teachers.

Education during British rule was limited to some sections of society. Indians who used to contribute regularly to the school funds promptly withdrew their monthly subscription, thinking that the low caste school was not in need of financial help". In the days of company's rule, Shudras were not encouraged to get education. Jyotirao's chain of schools meant for Dalit and Shudra girls and boys was just a humble beginning, but the functioning, management and the results attracted more and more sympathizers. There were orthodox people also who had opposed his venture. His upper caste friends helped him financially in running these schools. His efforts were symbolic for future generations. H.W. Reeves, then Revenue Commissioner, Southern Division, announced a donation of Rs. 15 per mensem for the schools of Mahars and Mangs. It can be seen from this that Jyotirao's work for the low castes were appreciated more by the liberal Europeans. The Europeans generously contributed towards the fund for the low caste schools.

He wrote the book *"Slavery"* in this book he described "I shall never forget the assistance H. W Reeves, Revenue Commissioner, rendered to the schools. He not only rendered financial help but also visited off and, on the Mahar-Mang schools, made inquiries about the progress made by them and struggled hard to encourage them in every way. Low caste people will be under his everlasting obligations which it would not be possible for them to repay. I am exceedingly grateful to various other Europeans who helped me in the spread of education among the Mahars and Mangs".

The status and position acquired by the schools established by Phule was good, but the question of earning a livelihood was pressing hard on him as both Jyotirao and his wife Savitribai had been serving the schools without any remuneration, nobly and selflessly. He passed some years fully engrossed in this work, which demanded close and unremitted attention. His father had driven him out of his house and he now felt the need of a job. He accepted the post of a teacher in a Scottish Missionary School in Pune. According to Mahatma Phule, if the Shudras and the ignored ones were educated, they will rise in revolt for their rights in society and establishing a just social order. Prayers and devotional songs were all for spiritual bliss. Education was for a rightful place in society. Phule found an opportunity to place the exact picture of negligible education among the Shudras when British Government appointed an Education Commission known as Hunter Commission. The Indian Education Commission appointed by the Government of India in 1882 was touring all over India. It was popularly known as *Hunter Commission* after its President Sir William Hunter. In every British Indian Province, a Provincial Committee was set up to help the Commission by giving it detailed information on the educational conditions. The

Commission studied the problem in every province and examined it. Memorials were addressed to the Commission and one of them was from Jyotirao.

Jyotirao stated that primary education was utterly neglected in the Bombay Presidency. Primary schools were not provided with proper requirements. Nearly nine-tenths of the villages in this Presidency or nearly 10 lakhs of children, it is said, are without any provision whatever for primary education. The cultivating and other poor classes, Jyotirao observed, did not avail themselves of the primary education. A few of the latter classes were found in primary and secondary schools, but they could not continue long in school because they were extremely poor; they required their children to tend cattle and to look after their fields; and they received no inducements in the forms of scholarships and prizes.

Concerning the system of Government scholarships, Jyotirao said that it should be so arranged that some of the scholarships should be awarded to those classes among whom education had made no progress. The system of awarding student's scholarships by competition, he added, although abstractedly equitable, did not tend to the spread of education among the poor classes.

Phule pleaded that, "primary education of the masses should be made compulsory up to a certain age, say at least 12 years. Muslims also hold aloof from these schools as they somehow evince no liking for Marathi or English. There are a few Muslim primary schools where their own language is taught. The Mahars, Mangs and other lower classes are practically excluded from all schools owing to caste prejudices, as they are not allowed to sit by the side of the children of the higher castes. Consequently, special schools for these have been opened by Government but they exist only in large towns. In the whole of Poona and for a population exceedingly over 5,000 people there is only one school in which the attendance is under 30 boys. This state of matters is not at all creditable to the educational authorities. I beg to urge that Mahars, Mangs and other classes, where their number is large enough, should have separate schools for them, as they are not allowed to attend the other schools owing to caste prejudices".

Jyotirao further said that the primary education imparted in Government schools must be placed on a satisfactory, sound basis, must be practical and useful in the future life of the children. Both the teaching machinery employed and the course of instruction then followed required a thorough remodelling. He was in favour of bettering the service conditions of teachers and recommended an increase in the salaries and status of the primary teachers, and also the appointment of trained teachers.

Throughout the text of *Gulamgiri*, Phule stresses that Hindu religion is indefensible mainly because it violates the rights and dignity of human beings. He turns the "false books" of the Brahmans on their head by reinterpreting the *"Dashavatara"* of Vishnu to rewrite a history of the struggles of the Shudras and Atishudras. He moves swiftly between the power and knowledge nexus in everyday cultural practices, myths and history. In his "Memorandum Addressed to the Education Commission" (1882) for a more inclusive policy on education and in his popular compositions like the short ballad on "Brahman Teachers in the Education Department" (1869), Phule demonstrates how state policy and dominant pedagogical practices are intrinsically interlinked. He comments at length on the differential treatment to children of different castes and the collusion of interests of the Bombay government school inspectors and teachers. He calls for more plurality in the appointment of teachers and the need to appoint those committed to teaching as a truth-seeking exercise.

Jyotirao's unflagging industry, perennial love and watchful care improved the tone of his schools, and these surpassed the work and worth of the Government. A note in the *Poona Observer* criticised the Board of Education for neglecting the Government Vernacular Schools and omitting one of their important and responsible duties.

It brought to their notice the deplorable condition of those schools which were put under the management of superannuated ill-educated men utterly ignorant of their duties. The guardians, it added, were exceedingly apathetic and the Government schools suffered for want of proper equipment. Contrasting the work of these Governments' vernacular schools with that of the female schools started by Jyotirao, a native friend of the editor of the *Poona Observer,* wrote to him that the attendance in those schools was ten times more numerous than that of the vernacular schools.

According to Phule, children were the wealth of the nation and the wealth of the nation was his wealth. He looked after the children in the orphanage opened by him. For money he had no love. He tried to live by his own hard work, never leaned on others for his livelihood. For ages it was the practice of the Shudras who rose to eminence by virtue of their learning or abilities to join the higher classes, to assimilate themselves with the Brahmins and to forget and neglect the class from which they sprang. Almost all Indian ancient famous saints and seers afford such illustrations. But Jyotirao was the only eminent man from the lower classes who had ample opportunities to attain prosperity and to shine in the galaxy of the brilliant men of the upper classes, and yet he neither joined them nor made common cause with them. The education and welfare of the lower classes absorbed his thoughts.

Realizing the work of Phule in education, the Bombay Guardian newspaper appreciated that, "…many of the old school Brahmins are displeased that a present of shawls should have been made to a Sudra (Govindrao is a gardener by caste, although not by occupation) the Brahmins maintain that a man of his rank should receive the lower reward of money. Probably the feeling is that of displeasure that any reward whatever should have been given to him. We have the pleasure of knowing well the energetic native of whom we have been writing. Were all young Poona like him, it would be a matter of exceeding joy. Probably we may have occasion to notice him again, ere long. To have to chronicle such things is a delightful task".

Jyotirao's colleagues were motivated by humanitarian ideals as were the English humanitarians of their age. But a humanitarian may not necessarily cherish a love for social and religious equality. This was the difference between Jyotirao and his benevolent colleagues. A man who inwardly clings to the idea of superiority of his high caste over others, from which he derives social prestige, privileges and power, cannot be a social revolutionary. Socially, a Brahmin cannot be a social revolutionary, barring some brilliant individual examples of great men, just as a British king cannot be a socialist by instinct. Jyotirao wanted to impart education in such a way that the lower classes would be prepared to fight for their rights of liberty and equality. At this time, some differences of opinion appeared to have arisen between them on the content and nature of education to be imparted to low caste children. The girls' schools started by Jyotirao were running smoothly under the management of the committee. He observed that he also requires certain reasons to place the schools for the Mahars and Mangs under a committee.

Now that Jyotirao had placed all the schools under societies, in the conduct of these schools the will of the majority came to prevail-Jyotirao's colleagues did not like the interpretations he put on the holy *puranas,* scriptures and history and were afraid these would filter down to the lower caste pupils. He bitterly exposed the motives of the makers of laws and social injunctions. The matter was discussed at some meetings and many differences came to the surface. Jyotirao insisted their colleagues that there should be such an education as would give them knowledge of what was right and what was wrong. He wanted them to fight for their rights and be able to guard their interests.

Jyotirao was honoured in consideration of the great interest he had taken in the establishment of native female schools in Poona for low caste children. It was indeed a great day for Jotirao's friends who, amidst stress and storm, heroically stood by him. It was also a great day in the history of female education and education of backward classes in India.

Jyotirao had been preparing the ground for a social reform movement. With a view to freeing the lower classes and caste-feeling and from the thraldom of Brahminism, he had written books and pamphlets on the subject. He was busy writing a book, parts of which he completed in August and December 1872. The first part of the book contained his proclamation under which he challenged Parashuram to appear before society as he was described by Brahmin scriptures and Puranas to have been living for ages. This was unmistakably a dig Jyotirao had at the Brahmins as he wanted to annihilate the doctrine of incarnation in Brahmanism.

The other part comprised his manifesto relating to his readiness to regard any man as a member of his family and to have food with him if he was convinced that the man led a virtuous life, had faith in God and was following an honest calling. Jyotirao declared that he himself had broken the shackles imposed upon him by Brahmin scriptures and come out of the prison of slavery. He denounced all Brahmin scriptures and their teaching which had condemned the Shudras as the slaves of Brahmins, and he declared as his brothers all those who treated him as his equal, even if from another country.

It was a sequel to his three books on the same subject. Liberty, equality, and fraternity is the burden of his books. Liberty is essential to every man. Tobestow, the book observes, liberty on a man who does not enjoy it is the duty of every good man under the sun. It is a great achievement to recapture the God-given rights of every human being who has been deprived of it. A self-respecting man would not falter to do this act. Every human being needs proper rights for his or her happiness. To confer freedom on every human being by liberating him from injustice, is the main object of noble men who undertake such great tasks at the risk of their lives.

Phule urged the necessity of nominating men from the lower classes to Municipal bodies to look after the interests and amenities of the lower classes, such as adequate supply of water and light. It was his experience that because of absence of representatives of the lower classes on Municipal bodies. The poor classes were not provided even the minimum supply of water. When the Atishudras and the poor classes of Poona started using cisterns in the localities of the Brahmins, they obtained a supply of water for their own cisterns. He felt that it was the bounden duty of the Municipality to provide proper lighting and an adequate water supply to the lower classes.

Phule revolted against priest craft, the gods of the Brahmins, the scriptures, *the puranas* as he thought they were dripping with tears and the blood of generations of Shudras and Atishudras who had been their victims for ages. British rule had brought with its justice, an independent judiciary, and scientific outlook, and stood in bold relief against the background of unrest, arson and injustice of Peshwa rule. He was happy to see that British rule had brought education, science and justice for all; but he overrated its blessings. He could not realize that the British god of Progress was sitting on the Indian caste system from which he did not care to alight, and so there would be no equitable progress for all the classes in India.

Jyotirao's fight for the emancipation of Shudras and Atishudras, who were peasants and landless classes, was against their exploiters, and in those day, they happened to be Brahmins. The men who were running the administration of the British were almost all Brahmins. The moneylenders and Government officers such as police-officers, *Shirastedars,* Mamlatdars and Assistant Judges were Brahmins. They all combined to keep the lower classes in bondage and exploited them jointly. Brahmin priests, money-lenders and lawyers were always there in every village to fleece them of money. Their lands and property were defrauded by this trio. So, the fight assumed the colour of communalism, though its trend was economic and social.

Jyotirao decided to set up an organization to preach his ideology. Accordingly, Jyotiba Phule convened on September 24, 1873, a meeting of all his admirers and disciples at Poona. About sixty men from many important centres of Maharashtra assembled. Jyotirao made an impressive introductory speech and impressed upon his followers the necessity of a central institution for the guidance of the movement. After some discussion and several other speeches, it was agreed to form an institution. There was much enthusiasm among the chosen lieutenants of Jyotirao. They decided to organise the mission and to spread the message of the movement. Jyotirao named this institution Satya-Shodhak Samaj (Truth-Seeking Society). It must be mentioned here that Phulr's three Brahmin friends, Vinayak Bapuji Bhandarkar, Vinayak Bapuji Dengle and Sitaram Sakharam Datar helped Jyotirao and his colleagues to establish the Satya-Shodhak Samaj.

The objects of the Samaj were to redeem the Shudras and Atishudras from the influence of Brahmanical scriptures under which the Brahmin priests fleeced them, to make them conscious of their human rights, and to liberate them from mental and religious slavery. Membership of the Samaj was extended to all castes including Brahmins and Mahars and Mangs, and even Jews and Muslims were its members in its early stage. The weekly meetings held on Sundays at the places where branches of the Satya Shodhak Samaj were established. The subjects discussed were the necessity of temperance and compulsory education, encouragement of swadeshi goods, dislodging the Brahmin priest from the position he held in the religious field, making arrangements for performing marriage at minimum expenses, and freeing men from the beliefs in astrology, ghosts and demons. The main attack was upon the caste system and idol-worship. Emphasis was also on the principle of the fatherhood of God and the brotherhood of Man.

Rationality and the equality were the principles on which he based the Satya Shodhak Samaj. The former principle was used to overthrow tradition and deny the supremacy of the scriptures. The principle of equality was used to attack the caste system. The Satya Shodhak Samaj worked to undermine the cultural and religious sanction for priest hood by conducting rituals and ceremonies without Brahmins. In its attack on the caste system it drew from both

Western rationalism as well as indigenous sources of social revolt like the Bhakti. What distinguished the Satya Shodhak Samaj was its non-elitist mass nature. In propagating its ideology, it made wide use of the vernacular. The backbone was the Maharastra peasantry (Maratha Kunbis, Malis, Kolis etc.). It also gained some support from untouchables. The "commercial bourgeoisie" comprising of tradesmen, contractors etc. were another source of support.

Jyotirao's activities were extended beyond the field of education. The drinking water tank in his house was thrown open to untouchables. This would be considered a brave act even today. In 1868, it was revolutionary. He believed that revolutionary thought has to be backed by revolutionary praxis.

Jyotirao Phule's exposure to education is important. He studied in one of the Scottish mission schools in Pune. The school was Phule's first encounter with new ideas of social reform and religious radicalism. The Scottish missionaries had a certain determination to admit boys of the lowest castes and this led to conflicts with Brahmin students. This intermingling of castes as well as the atmosphere of hostility left their imprint on Phule.

Phule suggested compulsory, universal and creative education. Education of women and the lower caste; he believed, deserved priority. Hence at home he began educating his wife Savitribai and open girl's first school in India in August 1848. Only eight girls were admitted on the first day. Steadily the number of students increased. Jyotirao opened two more girl's schools during 1851-52. He also started a school for the lower classes, especially the Mahars and Mangs. Thus, the pioneering work done by Phule in the field of female and lower castes education was unparalleled in the history of education in India. Phule was the first Indian social reformer who repeatedly urged the alien government to pay attention to primary education which was neglected. At that time, he was making people aware about the education and compelling the British Government to make arrangement for education of all people of India. He fought for the right of education equally for all the people regardless of the caste and class. He knew once the people are educated, they would fight themselves for their rights without any outside help and support. He said that progress of individuals was possible only with education. "The education which does not help the common mass of people to equip themselves for the struggle for life, which does not bring out strength of character, a spirit of philanthropy, and the courage of a lion…. real education is that which enables one to stand on one's legs". In the curriculum of primary education, preliminary knowledge about agriculture and health should be included. The curriculum of primary education should be reoriented to provide the demands of rural areas. There should be clear demarcation between the curriculum of rural and urban area. Education should be utilitarian and practical so as to cover the needs of the society. A scheme of ideal farming should be implemented on a small scale. Practical knowledge is superior to bookish knowledge hence primary knowledge in Modi (special Marathi scrip with regional languages supported), Accounts, History, Grammar, Agriculture, Ethics and Health should be imparted. Quantitative growth in Primary school is no doubt important but it should not be considered at the cost of qualitative one. Jyotiba Phule started two institutions- Native Female School, Pune and the Society for Promoting the Education of Mahars and Mangs. They built a network of schools in the Pune region through these two institutions. Phule started publication of two newspapers - *Dnyanodaya* and *Bombay Guardian* for extension of their efforts of female education and empowerment of backward classes.

Jyotirao Phule emphatically laid down on education. He emphatically laid down the lack of education as the root cause of the degradation of lower castes, as stated previously. "Mahatma Jyotirao Phule stressed on universalization of education i.e. education for all irrespective of caste, colour, creed, sex and poverty. Mahatma Jyotirao Phule had done a lot in his life to reform society, to fight for establishing equality in society. As he wanted education for all, same is the motto of present education system, to provide education to all. Following his principles Dr. Ambedkar had compiled the constitution in which we have provision for free and compulsory education and universalization of education in the constitution in the art 45 but the target of this article is yet to be achieved which was to be achieved within 10 years from the commencement of the constitution".

Many of the children were engaged in child labour in domestic households, agricultural fields and small-scale industries. But Phule and ruler of Kolhapur state, Shahu Maharaj established child rehabilitation centres and orphan houses and diverted children from being labour. Mahatma Phule was a follower of three famous Principles of namely equality, fraternity and brotherhood. Mahatma Phule wished all-round development of the society. The Satya Shodhak Samaj was the first institution to spread education among the backward and suppressed classes in rural area of Maharashtra. In 1848 he established first girl's school in Pune and made his wife Teacher. Even British Government admired his courage.

The activities of the Satya Shodhak Samaj got a fillip when the Maharaja of Kolhapur, Shahu Maharaja extended his support to it. The Maharaja had realized that political power was also necessary for advancement of the backward classes. To this end he encouraged the education of the lower castes and introduced reservation for them in his administration. Following Mahatma Phule he aided in replacing religious ceremonies which previously were the prerogative of Brahmins by those performed by the lower castes themselves. His initiatives set off a broad and very active movement of the lower castes which was to have a profound effect upon the growth of political organization in the Bombay Presidency and the shaping of the nationalist movement towards the end of the nineteenth century. He worked in the fields of Caste system, education particularly for women and lower castes, removal of untouchability and upliftment of widows.

Today education has been reduced to transmitting information. There is afear of examination because of bookish education. Little bit we have to be practical in system, we have to brought life-oriented education. In this context, Phule's education system is still very relevant. For him knowledge was not just information. It involves questioning, understanding critiquing knowledge. From the above discussion, we can understand that, Phule emphasized the education of Shudras, Ati-Shudras and women to get liberate themselves from the conventional shackles. For this purpose, he started female and Dalits' education. His ideas were based on humanity, equality and fraternity rather than blind faith. Even he has taken measures to eradicate practice of untouchability. His ideas were based on truth rather than blind faith and conventions. For this purpose, education is major way to get wisdom and knowledge and Phule encouraged education of these groups. Apart from education, Phule also organized his movement against untouchability. Further, he supported and encouraged widow remarriage.

Relevance of Jyotirao's Educational Philosophy Today

In today's educational scenario Phule's thoughts on education are very relevant. As we know, today education has been mostly reduced to information transmission. There is always a fear of examination because of bookish education. But for Phule knowledge was not just information, but it involves questioning, understanding critiquing and interpreting knowledge. As early as in the 19th century Phule had given alternative education models. For him, 'Education is the power to think clearly, the power to act well in the world's work, and the power to appreciate life'. For Phule knowledge matters because it can question, change and transform the individual and society. Education can empower and make society more democratic. It can help in reconstructing, rethinking and in interpreting tradition. This thought of Phule is extremely relevant in the paradoxical context of caste in contemporary India- where despite constitutional provisions, caste discrimination is widespread.

Jyotirao Phule was the first Indian educationist whose pragmatic views on education were honoured by the British rulers in India. He was a practical man with a profound philosophical background. The Indian educationists of his period and after were deeply impressed by the richness and originality of Phule's thoughts. His educational ideas and principles especially in the field of women's education and universal, free and compulsory primary education are most relevant in modern Indian society as elsewhere. It is not an exaggeration to say that the history of women's education in India would be incomplete without making a reference to the contribution of Mahatma Jyotirao Phule. He is rightly called Mahatma.

Conclusion

In the social and educational history of India, Mahatma Jyotirao Phule stands out as an exceptional personality. He was engaged in a passionate struggle to build a movement for equality between men and women and for social justice. Recognising that knowledge is power and that the progress of women and lower castes was impossible without it, he dedicated his entire life for spreading education. An Educational Philosopher among many thinkers and theorists one come across in the field of education, Jyotiba Phule was the first who devoted his life for the cause of mass education, the education of backward communities and women. His thoughts and ideas were revolutionary. His single most concern was universalization of primary education. He concentrated on such aspects as the need for primary education, the essential qualities to be possessed by primary school teachers and the curriculum of primary education. He gave importance to the upliftment of lower castes and women through education and took necessary steps for achieving this end. During Phule's time education for women and those born into castes considered untouchable was like a distant dream. In such a situation he launched a momentous struggle for the education of women and lower castes, in spite of threats to his life. For him education was not just literacy but a tool of social change in real sense of the term. He was the forerunner of Dr. B.R. Ambedkar as far as education of the downtrodden is concerned. For this reason, Dr. Ambedkar considered Mahatma Phule his "Guru". To Mahatma Phule education is the only panacea for eradicating social evils. It was his firm conviction that if social reforms are to be effective and lasting, persons at all levels should be educated. For this purpose, he considered the spread of education as his life's mission. Without doubt we can say that Phule was the pioneer of revolutionary thinking. He was rightly called the 'Father of Indian Social Revolution' in the modern age.

In 1848 Phule began his work as a social reformer. Interested in education of boys and girls of lower castes, he started a school for them. Since no female teacher was available, Phule asked his wife Savitribai to teach in the school. He opened two more schools for girls in 1851. He was honoured by the Board of education for the work he did for girls' education in 1852. Phule established a school for untouchables and a night school in 1852. By 1858, he gradually retired from the management of these schools and entered the broader field of social reform. He supported the movement for widow remarriage in 1860 and in 1863 established a Home for the prevention of infanticide. In a memorial addressed to the Education Commission popularly known as the Hunter Commission in 1882, he described his activities in the field of education. The government appointed him a member of the Poona Municipality in 1876. He continued as a member till 1882 and the concentration of the British Government was on higher education rather than on primary education. Though Jyotirao Phule was not against higher education, he was of the firm opinion that the common masses were less connected to higher education. Their urgent need was primary education that had relevance to their lives. He wanted educated persons of high vision and intellect to direct their attention towards ensuring humanism in education. He was against the traditional view that education should be used as an instrument for mass exploitation. Jyotirao Phule was a visionary who was also interested in educational policies. Therefore, in a statement presented to the Hunter Commission, he argued: "The present number of educated men is very small in relation to the country at large and we trust that the day may not be far distant when we shall have the present number multiplied a hundredfold - all taking themselves to useful and remunerative occupation not looking after service (Hunter Commission 1882)". Through education Phule was not just interested in temporarily raising the standard of living for a few persons. He was, in fact, thinking of the future of education for an independent India. His goal was to give Indian society an education that would not only have a permanent value, but also cultivate in the people a free mind and liberty of action.

Jyotirao Phule concentrated on the fact that the two important needs of an effective system of primary education were 'quality teachers' and a 'good curriculum'. In his view a primary teacher plays a pivotal role in the education process. According to Jyotirao Phule a primary teacher must be a trained person receiving sufficient salary. He wanted teachers to be drawn from lower castes so that they could be given employment opportunities. Phule was also of the view that efficient primary school teachers should be paid more salary than others. Mahatma Jyotiba Phule related education with access to justice, equity and growth for lower castes and women and asserted that only through education growth could be possible. Phule's thoughts on education can be summarised as follows: "Lack of education leads to lack of wisdom, which in turn leads to lack of justice. This leads to lack of progress, which leads to lack of money and results in oppression of the lower castes".

Mahatma Phule was fully conscious about the importance of education as a tool of social justice and equality. In fact, he saw education as the harbinger of a social revolution. The essence of the educational philosophy of Mahatma Phule was that 'education is a human right'. He was indeed the protagonist of the ides of universalization of educational opportunities. Universalization of education basically means accepting and extending facilities of education to all irrespective of caste, creed, religion, sex and physical or moral disability. Indian Constitution is the symbol of victory for the philosophy of equality of educational opportunity propounded by Mahatma Phule.

He also worked for education of women and virtually laid the foundation for opening up opportunities for women to seek formal education. This was especially true of women from the marginalised sections. For achieving his aims, he opened a girl's school in 1848 at

BudhwarPeth in the residential building of Tatya Sahib Bhide. He opened two more schools in 1851 among which one school was for girls of backward class. He had revolutionary ideas about different aspects of education.

Since all human beings are equal, access to education must be uniform. Monopolistic controls over education must be curtailed. Universalization of opportunities and compulsory education must be ensured. While educating individuals, religion, race, caste and sex should not be considered. Education should develop humanistic values. The education of women and other deprived groups must be given top priority for establishment of social justice. Education must serve as a binding force in society. A primary school teacher must be a trained person and sufficient salary should be paid to him/her. Curriculum must be utilitarian and practical so as to cover the needs of the society. Preliminary knowledge about agriculture and health should be included in the curriculum. There should be a differentiation between the curriculum of rural and urban schools. Values that stand the test of time such as freedom, equality, fraternity, kindness, self-respect, devotion to one's nation and internationalism should be developed through education.

Professional ability and efficiency should be developed so that knowledge may be properly linked. The downward filtration theory advocated by Lord Macaulay is not philosophically sound as it ignores the common masses. The practical knowledge is superior to bookish knowledge. Hence primary knowledge in Modi (a special Marathi script) accounts, history, grammar, agriculture ethics and health should be imparted. Though, quantitative growth in primary schools is important, it should not be at the cost of qualitative growth. The government must formulate the scheme of scholarships and rewards for deserving students and those in need of support.

Phule's bold efforts to educate women, Shudras and the untouchables had a deep effect on the values, beliefs and ideologies relating to the movement for social justice through education. His efforts unleashed the forces of awakening among the common masses. Education made women more knowledgeable. They became conscious of the differences between the right and the wrong and could analyse these differences with a scientific approach. They began to question the age-old customs which degraded them. Similarly, Shudras started claiming equality with upper castes in all areas of life. In short, Jyotirao Phule launched a movement for liberating women and Shudras from the control of vested interests and laid the foundation for a Backward Class Movement in India.

REFERENCES

1. Ahuja, Ram (1993). *Indian Social System*. Jaipur: Rawat Publications.

2. Altekar, A.S (1962). *Position of Women in Hindu Civilization: Prehistoric Times to the Present Day*. New Delhi: Motilal Banaras idass.

3. Ambedkar, B.R (1946). *Who Were the Shudras? How They Came to Be the Fourth Varna in the Indo-Aryan Society*. Bombay: Thacker and Company.

4. Archana Kumari & Shweta Gautam (2015). *Human Rights: Violation of Women in India*, 2(7)

5. Bakane, Chhaya, et al., (2012), Contribution of Jyotiba Phule (1827-1890), in *Modern Indian Political Thought*. Chhaya Bakane et al. (Eds.), Mumbai, University of Mumbai,.

6. Basham, A.D. (1971). *The Wonder that was India*. Calcutta: Rupa and Company.

7. Batra, Manjula, (2008). *Protection of Human Rights in Justice Administration: A Study of the Rights of Accused in India and Soviet Union*. New Delhi: Deep and Deep Publications.

8. Bhole, B.L. (2002). *Jyotiraonchi Samata-Sankalpan*. Mumbai: Lokvangmay Grih.

9. Bhole, B.L. (2009). *Mahatma Jyotirao Phule: Warsa Aani Wasa*. Aurangabad: Saket Prakashan.

10. Borawake, Kranti Suhas (2017), *Contribution of Savitribai Phule in the field of Education*, Vidyawarta, Special Issue, pp. 06-09.

11. Chanchreek, K.L. (2006). *Social Reform Movement and Jyotiba Phule*. New Delhi: Shree Publishers and Distributors.

12. Chatrath, K.J.S. (1998). *Education for Human Rights, and Democracy.* Shimla: Indian Institute of Advanced Study.

13. Chauhan, C.P.S. (2011). Participation of Women in Higher Education: The Indian Perspective, *Analytical Reports in International Education,* 4(1), pp. 67-86.

14. Chausalkar, A. (2001). Mahatma Phuleani Shetkari Chalwal, *Mahatma Phule and the Peasant Movement.* Mumbai: Lok Vangmaya Griha.

15. Coser, L. (2010), *Masters of Sociological Thoughts Ideas in Historical and Social Context.* New Delhi: Rawat Publications.

16. Deshmukh, C.L. (2015). *Socio-Legal Perspective of Shahu*, Phule, Ambedkar on the Child Labour, *Research Front*, Special Issue No. 16, pp. 91-92.

17. Deshpande, G.P. (1989). *Satyashodhak.* Aurangabad: Saket Prakashan.

18. Deshpande, G.P. (2002). *Introduction to Selected Writings of Jyotirao Phule.* New Delhi: Leftword.

19. Dumont, L. (1970). *Homo Hierarchicus: The Caste System and Its Implication.* Chicago: University of Chicago Press.

20. Faizal, T. K. (2017). *Mahatma Jyotirao Phule: Enlightened Reformer of Indian Education. Vidyawarta*, Special Issue, pp. 09-11.

21. Gail Omvedt (2001). *Phule and Women's Libseration.* Mumbai: Lok Vangmaya Griha.

22. Gail Omvedt, (2006). *The Anti-Caste Movement and the Construction of an Indian Identity.* New Delhi: Orient Longman Private Limited.

23. Gaur, A. (1980). *Women in India.* London: The British Library Series.

24. Gavli, P.G. (1988). *Society and Social Disabilities under the Peshwas.* New Delhi: National Publishing House.

25. Ghosh, G.K. and Ghosh, S. (1997). *Dalit Women.* New Delhi: A.P.H. Publishing Corporation.

26. Ghurye, G.S. (2008). *Caste and Race in India.* Bombay: Popular Prakashan.

27. Gupta, N.L. (2008). *Mahatma Jotiba Phule an Educational Philosopher.* New Delhi: Anmol Publications Pvt. Ltd.

28. Hosamani, S.H. (2015), *Mahatma Jyotibha Phule's Concept of Social Justice, Ph.D Thesis*, Gulbarga University.

29. Jagtap, M. (1993). *Yugpurusha Mahama Phule.* Bombay: Mahatma Phule Chavitra Sadhane Prakashan Samitee.

30. Jaswal, P., et al. (1996). *Human Rights and the Law*. New Delhi: APH Publishing Corporation.

31. Joshi, T.L. (2013). *Jotirao Phule*, Translated by Daya Agarwal, New Delhi, National Book Trust.

32. Kadam, S. (2008), Mahatma Phule Aani Mahatrashtratil Rajkaran. Aurangabad: Chinmay Prakashan.

33. Keer, D. (2013). *Mahatma Jotirao Phooley*. Mumbai: Popular Prakashan.

34. Kosari, R. (2016), An Overview Status of Literacy among Rural Andhra Pradesh, *Journal of Applied Management Science*, 2(11), pp. 1-8.

35. Kuppuswamy, B. (2002). *Social Change in India*, Bangalore: Prasaranga, Bangalore University.

36. Low, D.A. (1987). Caste, Conflict, and Ideology. *Mahatma Jotirao Phule and Low Caste Protest in Nineteenth-Century Western India* by Rosalind O'Hanlon, *Modern Asian Studies*, 21(1), p. 206-208.

37. Mahesh, Thakur, & Kumar, A. (2015). Social Justice in India and Contribution of Various People in the Upliftment of Dalits, *International Journal of Multidisciplinary and Current Research*, 3(1), pp. 105-106.

38. Begum, M. (2000). *Human Rights in India*. New Delhi: APH Publishing Corporation.

39. Islam, M. (2013). *Feminism: Conceptual and Ethical Issues*. New Delhi: Mittal Publications.

40. Mishra, S. (2002). *Status of Indian Women*. New Delhi: Gyan Publishing House.

41. Mukherjee, R. (1986). *Caste, Conflict and Ideology: Jotirao Phule and Low Caste Protest in Nineteenth-Century Western India* by Rosalind O'Hanlon, Social History, 11(3), p. 399-401.

42. Narake, H. (1982). Mahatma Phule Gaurav Granth, Mumbai: Maharashtra State Government Publication.

43. Narake, H. (2008). On Savitribai Phule: Dnyanajyoti Savitribai Phule, Savitribai Phule Lecture Series, edited by T. Sundararaman, New Delhi: NCERT.

44. NUEPA (2014). *Towards Quality with Equity India*. New Delhi: MHRD

45. O'Hanlon, Rosalind (1985). *Caste, Conflict and Ideology*. Cambridge: Cambridge University Press.

46. Palekar, S.A. (1997). *Concept of Equality and Ideal Society*. New Delhi: Rawat Publications

47. Palekar, S.A. (2010). Basaveshwara and Human Rights. Jaipur: ABD Publishers.

48. Parmar, Y.S. (1973). Polyandry in the Himalayas. Delhi: Vikas Publishing House.

49. Patil, Sharad. (1987). *Slavery of Daasas and Shudras*. Wari: Prajna Press.

50. Pawar, A.D. (2014), The Study of Social and Educational Work of Mahatma Phule, *PhD Thesis*, Jhunjhunu, Rajasthan, Shri Jagdishprasad Jhabarmal Tibrewala University.

51. Phadke, Y.D. (1991). *Collected Works of Mahatma Phule.* edited by Dhananjay, K. & S.G. Malshe, Mumbai: Maharashtra Rajya Sahityaani Sanskriti Mandal.

52. Ponnian, M. (2000). *Education and Human Rights*. New Delhi: Ponnian Publications.

53. Prema, A. (2012). Women Status in India. *Indian Streams Research Journal*, 2(1)

54. Ragi, S.B., Bamman, & Jyoti, S. (2011). Mahatma Phule and Women's Emancipation, *Research Analysis and Evaluation*, p.114-115.

55. Rajni, B. & Navjoti (2012). Mahatma Jyoti Rao Phule: A Forgotten Liberator, *International Journal of Basic and Advanced Research*, 1(2), pp. 32-36.

56. Ralhan, O.P. et al. (1995). *Indian Women Through Ages*. New Delhi: Anmol Publications.

57. Raskar, B.R. (2015). The Study of the Economic Ideas of Mahatma Phule, *Ph.D Thesis*, Aurangabad, Dr. Babasaheb Ambedkar Marathwada University.

58. Renu, P. (2015). Crusaders of Female Education in Colonial India: A case study of Savitribai Phule, *International Journal of Innovative Social Science & Humanities Research,* 2(1), pp. 1-6.

59. Saini, D. (2014). Mahatma Jyotirao Phule and Peasants: A Historical Study, *Research Matrix: International Multidisciplinary Journal of Applied Research*, 1(6)

60. Saki (1998). Making History: Karnataka's People and their Past, Stone Age to Mercantilism, Bangalore: Vimukthi Prakashana.

61. Salunkhe, A.H. (2001). Mahatma Phule and Dharma (Phule and Dharma), Mumbai: Lok Vangmaya Griha.

62. Sardar, G.B. (2005). *Mahatma Phule: Vyaktitva Aani Vichar*. Mumbai: Granthali.

63. Rao, S. (1960). *Women in the Vedic Age*. Bombay: Bharatiya Vidya Bhawan.

64. Rao, C.N. (2006). *Indian Society*. Mangalore: Jai Bharat Publications.

65. Sharma, R.S. (1980). *Sudras in Ancient India: A Social History of the Lower Order Down to circa AD 600*. Delhi: Motilal Banarasidass.

66. Sharmila Rege (2010). Education as *Trutiya Ratna*: Towards Phule Ambedkarite Feminist Pedagogical Practice, *Economic & Political Weekly*, 45(44), pp. 88-98.

67. Sharma, G. (2000). *Human Rights and Social Justice*. New Delhi: Deep and Deep.

68. Somashekharappa, C.A. (2010): *Dalit Employee: A Sociological Study of Inter-Personal Relations at Work Place*. Jaipur: Prateeksha Publications.

69. Stephen (2012). *The Legacy Illiteracy: Ignorance is Expensive*. Bloomington: Authors House.

70. Sube S. (2015), Mahatma Govindrao Jotiba Phule and Satya Shodhak Samaj: A Social Reform Movement in Maharashtra in the Second Half of the Nineteenth Century, *Indian Journal of Applied Research*, 5(6), pp. 498-500.